BALANCE

THE JOURNEY TO BECOMING COMFORTABLE IN THE UNCOMFORTABLE

TIMOTHY T. MITCHELL

CONTENTS

FOREWORD

Growth rarely occurs in times of comfort, relaxation, or ease. Balance: The Journey to Being Comfortable with the Uncomfortable invites us to step beyond the security of the familiar and into the sacred space where God shapes, stretches, and strengthens us for greater purpose. If you're ready to grow in every area of your life, this book is for you.

Pastor Timothy Mitchell has done a masterful job of articulating how what we often consider "comfort" can actually hinder our growth. He helps us reframe discomfort—not as something to avoid, but as a divine invitation to grow. What we call "disruption," "stretching," or "discomfort" is often God's tool for transformation.

We live in a world that values routine, predictability, and the status quo. Yet life—and especially faith—consistently call us into seasons of uncertainty, challenge, and discomfort. The journey toward purpose, maturity, wholeness, and God's best always involves stepping into the unknown. Like a mother eagle that stirs the nest—removing the soft layers to expose thorns and twigs so her eaglets will learn to fly—God sometimes unsettles our comfort to awaken our wings. It's in these moments that we confront our fears, examine our assumptions, and take the leap of faith.

What I love about Balance is Pastor Tim's honesty, transparency, and wisdom. He doesn't just write these principles—he's lived them. In one of my favorite lines, Pastor Tim writes, "Balance is not about everything being even; it's about finding equilibrium between God's purpose for your life and your plans." That's a powerful and liberating truth.

As Pastor Tim's spiritual father and pastor for over 14 years, I've had the privilege of witnessing his personal, professional, and spiritual journey. From husband, father, and educator to leader and founding pastor of Intersection Church in the Dallas–Fort Worth area, his life is a testimony of what happens when we let God stir the nest. The growth hasn't always been easy, but Pastor Tim embraced the process—and God has honored his faith.

This book is more than just "a read"—it's a resource. It's a tool for anyone ready to be stretched, for any leader ready to be challenged, and for every believer ready to grow. I envision it being used in small groups, leadership teams, and personal development settings. Each chapter includes discussion questions to encourage reflection, application, and conversation.

Prepare to be challenged. Prepare to be changed. But most of all, prepare to be balanced—by grace, by courage, and by the God who does His greatest work when we step outside our comfort zones. Whether you're embracing new responsibilities, confronting personal limitations, learning to forgive, or simply sensing that God is calling you to more—this book

Timothy T. Mitchell

will meet you where you are and guide you toward who you are becoming.

This book blessed me. I know it will bless you.

Bishop Kevin K. Dickerson, MDiv.
PASTOR, DAYSPRING FAMILY CHURCH
PRESIDING PRELATE, VISION FELLOWSHIP OF CHURCHES

CHAPTER 1

HEALTHY CONVERSATIONS

. . . .

B*alance: The Journey to Becoming Comfortable in the Uncomfortable* is not just a collection of personal stories, spiritual truths, or motivational encouragements. It's a call to alignment. Each chapter explores a specific tension point in life: from managing your emotions and guarding your integrity to healing your identity, embracing the impossible, saying yes to God's will, and walking in radical forgiveness. The common thread is balance. Not a perfect equilibrium, but a holy rhythm that lets you grow through what once unsettled you. As you read, you'll be challenged to lean into reflection, apply timeless principles to real-time struggles, and build a life rooted in obedience, resilience, and grace. This journey isn't about removing the discomfort. It's about learning to thrive within it.

Do you realize that how you respond to certain matters in your life has the power to change everything? Think back to those moments in your life when you should have said that two-letter word: "No." How might it have changed your life for the better? A simple "no" can redirect the course of your life.

Always remember that for every hard choice you make, you are going to have a massive result. There will be a substantial shift in your story.

Genesis 3:6 says, *"And when the woman saw that the tree was good for food, and that it was pleasant to the eyes, and a tree to be desired to make one wise, she took of the fruit thereof, and did eat and gave also unto her husband with her; and he did eat."*

Nowhere in this verse is the serpent mentioned. At that moment, Eve is making a choice based on certain narratives she tells herself. Do you see a place in that verse where the serpent forced her? He simply asked some questions that unlocked something in Eve.

Before Eve ever touched the fruit, she told herself a narrative that was compelling, convincing, and undeniable. We often try to blame others for where we are, but at some point, you must recognize that you are the main character and narrator of your story. This verse is proof that Eve was her own enemy. Her desire became the main attraction. This is where I want to caution you.

TSA checks your bags before you load them on a plane to ensure that you are not carrying something that could be detrimental to yourself or others. They run your duffle bag through machines that give them a clear view of what's inside. Just as TSA checks bags for safety, you must check your heart's desires because therein lies the true driver of your life. Desire is a longing, a craving, and a lusting that will not rest until it finds a place to lay its head. It is a conscious pull toward something we believe will bring us joy or fulfillment once we attain it.

The key is to realize that you are conscious. It is an intrinsic inspiration and mental motivation that causes you to gravitate to a decision based on the story you're telling yourself. When you are narrating your own story, you can lose all sense of connection to what is sensible, discreet, wise, manageable, and most of all, akin to God's best for your life. Eve told a story about the fruit that contradicted what God said, and because she didn't check her desire, she disobeyed. Unchecked desire has the potential to give birth to disobedience.

The ability to say no when you really want to say "yes" boils down to foundational principles. If you can manage these principles, your ability to be self-disciplined, stay the course, and not be deterred by external circumstances will lead you to proper progression in life.

PRINCIPLE #1 –
KNOW THYSELF IN CONVERSATION!

You must understand that questions unlock something in you. If you are speeding and you enter a speed check area, you run the risk of being pulled over by an officer. The officer always asks for license and registration. They want to identify you and the vehicle that you are driving before they issue you a warning, or God forbid, a ticket.

Identify yourself so that you don't lose yourself while enjoying the company of friends, family, and acquaintances. Conversation has a way of wetting your palate for the unknown. Just as the officer identifies you with the car, you must identify yourself before you walk into any room.

Integrity sometimes loses its grip during a conversation. Respect for your spouse can dissipate just by having a conversation. Discontentment on your job can increase based on your conversations. You are home for Thanksgiving and your sibling just bought a new home that is undeniably gorgeous. You overhear them talking to another family member about the splendor of their newly purchased home, and now, you're burning with envy.

God had a conversation with Cain about the sin that was knocking at his door. Cain was so consumed with rage and jealousy that he killed his innocent brother. Abel wasn't Cain's problem. Cain's violation had a direct correlation with him not knowing himself in conversation.

Before you walk into a room, tell yourself a story about who you are—your successes, your motivations, your objectives—and celebrate your progress. Remind yourself that you are enough and that you are on your own journey. Consequently, you will have the power to say no to the temptations of rage, jealousy, comparison, and discontentment because you've considered the value of your own life.

You will also be unyielding to the feeling of satisfaction that comes from the demise of another. Both are unhealthy. But because you know thyself in conversation, you've identified yourself, and you are telling yourself a narrative that is true about your life. This awareness keeps you from being sucked into the vacuum of disdain because of others' success.

Furthermore, God has a way of giving you a front-row seat to view the success of other people to provoke you to deal with your insecurities. Yes, you must confront those places in you that feel awkward when others are expressing how they are advancing in life. God has called us to be balanced! We shouldn't be antsy in our seats because our coworker got a promotion. Know yourself in conversation, and you can genuinely celebrate the success of others.

PRINCIPLE #2 –
KNOW WHAT YOU POSSESS!

The enemy is tricky and will try to sell you land that you already own. Luke 4:5–8 (KJV) says, *"And the devil, taking him up into a high mountain, shewed unto him all the kingdoms of the world in a moment of time. And the devil said unto him, All this power will I give thee, and the glory of them: for that is delivered unto me; and to whomsoever I will I give it. If thou therefore wilt worship me, all shall be thine. And Jesus answered and said unto him, Get thee behind me, Satan: for it is written, Thou shalt worship the Lord thy God, and him only shalt thou serve."*

This passage indicates the enemy's audacity, but it also reflects Jesus's understanding of what was truly important. Jesus was fully aware that He would learn obedience through suffering and that to accept the devil's invitation would disrupt the process necessary to prepare Him to sacrifice His life for mankind.

Jesus would have prematurely received what was already His if He had accepted the enemy's offer. Getting something early that is already yours is dangerous! You must choose the path with the highest level of resistance and keep moving forward. Otherwise, you become like the son in the Bible who demanded his inheritance and wasted it all. Be aware! There is a direct correlation between waste and immaturity. Jesus said "yes" to the process and "no" to prematurely receiving what He would ultimately gain upon resurrection day.

Furthermore, the devil was limited in what he could offer Jesus. The opportunity to obtain glory only on Earth? What God the Father had for Jesus was all power in Heaven and on Earth. When you make plans with the enemy and receive things early, you risk getting far less than you would have if you had stayed dedicated and loyal to the Father alone.

My prayer for you is to be steadfast, solid, and unmovable in saying "yes" to a journey with Jesus that will allow you to grow gracefully and receive what your God has already promised you. Eve saw the tree as one to be desired because it could make her wise, but she couldn't recognize that Wisdom showed up every day and spoke with her. Beautiful provisions were at her fingertips through the Father of wisdom. She already had possession of what was most important, yet she couldn't see it.

PRINCIPLE #3 –
KNOW THE COST OF YOUR "YES"!

Opportunity cost is what you give up when you choose one option over another. It's the value of the best alternative you didn't choose. The concept of opportunity cost is a calculation in your mind regarding channeling your energy from one area to another with the expectation that the new place of expenditure will afford you more than what you currently have.

Sometimes, more isn't truly more. Sometimes the choice between saying "yes" to one venture and saying "no" to another becomes more of a burden than a benefit. Genesis 16:2–3 says, *"Now Sarai Abram's wife bare him no children: and she had a handmaid, an Egyptian, whose name was Hagar. And Sarai said unto Abram, Behold now, the Lord hath restrained me from bearing: I pray thee, go in unto my maid; it may be that I may obtain children by her. And Abram hearkened to the voice of Sarai."*

Sarai suggested that Abraham sleep with her handmaiden, Hagar, to create a new life because she believed God would never allow her to conceive a child. Sarai saw an opportunity to have a child by other means, and she took it. But God made good on His promise, and whether we know it or not, our choices have the propensity to be at war with God's.

Despite God's promise of a child from her womb, Sarai didn't fight the temptation to resist this act. Because of her decision, she was now at war with a choice birthed from doubt and fear. What she thought was a good chance for progression and advancement became her worst nightmare.

Hagar's son, Ishmael (Sarai's idea), grew up with Sarai's son, Isaac (God's idea). For a while, it seemed fine, but at some point, God's promise was taunted by Sarai's bright idea. Sarai watched the boys interact and saw Ishmael mocking Isaac, and she became discontent with the arrangement. She demanded Abraham put Hagar and her son out.

Sarai didn't count the cost of saying "yes." Furthermore, in Scripture, Genesis 22:16 says, *"And said, By myself have I sworn, saith the Lord, for because thou hast done this thing, and hast not withheld thy son, thine only son."*

The Scripture goes on to tell Abraham how God would bless him because of his obedience, but that's not what I want to highlight. I want to highlight that God defined Isaac, the child He promised to Abraham and Sarai, as Abraham's only son.

This must not be overlooked, because God's ways, His moves, and His thoughts are not like ours. Sarai, not understanding the cost of her "yes," caused a son to be produced named Ishmael. Ishmael wasn't acknowledged by God in Genesis 22:16 because he was a product of a faithless move. I'm aware that Scripture shows God speaking to Hagar and taking care of her and Ishmael, but God only truly acknowledged Isaac as Abraham's son.

Saying "yes" to a bright idea without knowing how costly it could be is dangerous. Develop the strength to hold your ground, be resilient, and ignore the opportunities that merely *look* good. Let this season in your life be filled with joy and happiness while you wait for the Father to fulfill His promise in your life.

One day I was preparing to minister, and so many things were going wrong. We were about to go live in just a few minutes. I tried to keep my mind intact while I witnessed apathy, slothfulness, malfunctioning devices, and opinions being shot like arrows across the room from various sources. I was more frustrated than I could adequately describe. It was impressed upon me to put on my headphones and play a song called "Called to Be" by Jonathan Nelson. After listening to that song, I put another on repeat: "Trust Me" by Richard Smallwood. I played "Trust Me" up until the last minute before going online to minister.

I was walking around the church, just praying that nothing I saw would cause me to lose ground, lose my witness, or lose my opportunity to minister. During my time of turmoil, with my headphones on, trying to block out the noisy distractions of foolishness, I faced the wall, laid my hands on it, and began to pray.

God spoke to me, and He said, "It's just a moment!" When God spoke those words, I automatically took a deep breath, and His peace flooded my space. My heart was renewed. Saying "no" when you really want to say "yes" has a spiritual connotation to it. I hope you're catching it. Saying "no" requires self-discipline. Saying "no" requires you to be knowledgeable of God's promises in your life. Saying "no" affords you the opportunity to avoid God's promise having to war with your bright idea.

Do not yield to the temptation to sin. Work diligently to avoid the temptation to give everyone in the room a piece of your mind. Put the brakes on the thought that God needs your help. Become unyielding in your pursuit to obtain something that is already yours through focus and a good work ethic. Fight to say "no" so that you don't yield to a "yes" that will not be acknowledged by God because you didn't run it by Him first.

My prayer is that you dig in! My prayer is that, when it gets hard, you listen for the voice of God on how to block out all the noise, and don't forget: It's just a moment. Weeping may endure for a night, but joy comes in the morning. Let your "yes" be a God-yes, and let your "no" be a God-no. This is the first step to creating a healthy balance in your life. Balance requires a strong core, and only the strong will survive.

BALANCE BUILDER · · · · · · · · · · · · · · · · · ·

Healthy conversations are where transformation begins. When we examine our motives and speak the truth, we invite growth. Our words carry weight and using them with intention brings clarity and peace. Let your conversations reflect purpose and your values remain steady, even in tough moments.

Your words shape your world. These questions will help you uncover the power of your "yes," the weight of your "no," and the truth that healthy conversations often begin by being honest with yourself.

1. What desire or internal narrative have I failed to examine before making a major decision?

2. In what situations do I need to practice saying "no" to protect my purpose?

3. Have I ever chosen a "bright idea" over God's promise, and what was the cost?

4. How do I prepare myself mentally and spiritually before entering conversations that could shift my emotions?

5. What does it mean for me to walk with integrity, even when the room is full of noise?

CHAPTER 2

EMOTIONAL READINESS

. . . .

I have a cousin. We will call him J in this chapter. J and I grew up together, and we were like two peas in a pod. Many weekends I would go and stay over at his house, and we would compete in practically everything possible. Something as menial as making a peanut butter and jelly sandwich. Before our peanut butter bread slice married our jelly bread slice, we would compare to see who smoothed their peanut butter the best with the butter knife. I'm writing the book, and I have the mic, so I'll say my sandwich was the most aesthetically pleasing. Truth be told, I truly don't remember. I just remember that the excitement was embedded within the confines of competition.

Additionally, J and I would always carve out time to get side-by-side in the mirror to see who was the tallest. We needed to check this on a regular basis as we were both growing boys drinking lots of milk and eating multiple peanut butter and jelly sandwiches in a day. I believe that God has a sense of humor because my son Matthew has recently been forcing me to the mirror to assess the difference in our height. I must say that he's officially the tallest in the house now. I'm good with it. Subsequently, I've been through this before with my cousin J. My height hovered and sustained at 5 feet 10 inches. My cousin went on to tower over me at well over 6 feet tall. There was no longer a need to check. He stood out like a sore thumb.

J would go on to be head and shoulders over most, apart from one of his brothers that God endowed to be monstrously tall as well. J's brother has gone on to produce his own giant. I'm not bitter anymore. Sometimes God lets scenarios continue to live in your life until you are forced to deal with how you truly feel about that area in your life. I'm much better.

Initially, I struggled with my height. Naturally, I had no choice but to stop and come to grips with where my stature would halt. How ironic that God would allow me to have a son who would force me back to the mirror to discover once again that there was no competition. I love God for that. Could you add that to your prayer life? It's a tough ask but walk with me. Just say, "Lord, let me stay long enough where I am for the discontentment to die on the vine, and I truly discover the value that you locked up inside of me."

I tell this truth about my cousins and me for entertainment purposes. It truly is hilarious, and I promise, I'm okay. But what is genuinely a reverberation in many of our lives is that there are times we get stuck in the corridor of competition, stuck in the maze of amazement of others' qualities, stuck in the realm of someone's reality, and we miss that we are fearfully and wonderfully made by God.

I would like to take you on a journey as we travel through the mind of Cain. Yes, the Cain in Genesis that we alluded to in Chapter 1. I believe his interaction with his brother and his interaction with God scream food for thought and opportunistic value that will help guide us on the appropriate path to find balance in our emotions.

Currently, as I'm writing this book, we are into a new season of *American Idol*. It just started. My wife is a huge fan of the show, and she doesn't miss an episode. Look out! Stay out of her way. Shhhh, no talking at 7 PM on Sunday and Monday night. My wife comes with all her snacks and her blanket. For two hours, she becomes lost in the abyss of *American Idol*. Now, I cannot lie. I'm frequently in the same area, glued to the television, on the edge of my seat wondering whether *American Idol* wasted 5 minutes highlighting the story of an individual who couldn't sing if their life depended on it.

I've discovered the best *American Idol* contestants are those who realize that they are truly in competition with themselves. It is the contender who gets out of his or her way, finds freedom in expressing the essence of who they are, and their ability to become comfortable in their skin, who soar!

Are you comfortable in your skin? Do you like yourself? Do you see your value? How's your emotional aptitude? Quick note: it is often in very high-energy and challenging moments that you catch a glimpse of who you truly are. Your ability to be in control of your emotions in tough times, like an *American Idol* contestant, while under immense pressure, will assist you in nailing down your desired outcome.

Can you keep it together? Can you remember who you are? There is a quote by Viktor E. Frankl that says, "Between stimulus and response, there is a space. In that space lies our freedom and power to choose our response. In our response lies our growth and freedom."

You are as free as your ability to be in control of yourself. And your growth is evident in how you respond in tough times. Emotional intelligence refers to the ability to perceive, understand, and manage one's own emotions and relationships.

Jesus, the mentor of Peter, is taken in for questioning by the Roman government. Before this, Jesus was kissed on his cheek by the betraying disciple Judas who walked closely with him. As the Roman soldier apprehends Jesus, Peter pulls his sword and cuts off the ear of the servant of the high priest. The precision of Peter's aim must be noted. If we rewind the story, Peter, at a crucial time, was asleep when he should've been in prayer. Jesus, while having his own experience with the Father, was imploring Peter, James, and John to pray. I wonder if his first instinct was to cut off the servant's ear because of his lack of time in prayer.

There is a direct correlation between your prayer life and the precision of your decisions. Peter, in the moment that he cut off the servant's ear, shows how dull he was spiritually. He cut off the very body part of the servant that he should've been using to be his best self in the moment: the ear. In the second and third chapters of Revelation, a popular verse says, *"He that hath an ear, let him hear what the Spirit saith to the churches."*

Prayer would have made his spiritual ear sharp. Is it possible that we are sharpening the wrong weapons in our lives? We are sharper physically than we are spiritually because we spend more time on the areas that benefit us less. Sharpening our minds, hearts, thoughts, emotions, ideologies, and convictions will lead to more growth and overall well-being. Over time, Peter would grow to be sharper in his spiritual hearing.

This realization about sharpening the right weapons hit me deeply when I transitioned into two major life shifts—becoming the pastor of Intersection Church and stepping into the field of insurance after 14 years in education. Both experiences taught me that sharpening the right skills, the right mindset, and the right spirit would be crucial to thriving. I grew up in church all my life and witnessed firsthand what ministry looked like under the leadership of my father. For over ten years, I watched him build systems, support the community, and connect with other pastors. When I moved to the Dallas-Fort Worth area, I served at Dayspring Family Church in Irving, Texas, for 14 years under Bishop Dickerson and Pastor Sonja Dickerson. It was there that I learned how to run a large ministry with multiple services and how to build teams and leaders effectively. I saw what it took to manage conferences and events and even travel across the nation to minister the Word.

However, when God called me to pastor, I had to be conscious not to simply copy what I had seen. I learned from both my natural father's ministry and my spiritual father's ministry, but I knew I had to sharpen my spiritual hearing and lean into God's specific calling for Intersection Church. I couldn't be a copycat or a cookie-cutter representation of what I had seen. God was doing something unique, and I had to be sensitive enough to hear His voice and recognize the spiritual identity He was creating through me.

Similarly, when I transitioned from education to insurance, I felt the weight of it. I spent 14 years in education, building relationships, moving from teacher to administrator, and becoming deeply rooted in that field. Stepping into insurance meant I had to learn entirely new systems, structures, and directives. It was overwhelming. I found myself under immense pressure to perform and adapt quickly. During breaks, I would walk outside, take deep breaths, and remind myself why I was doing what I was doing. I had to sharpen my perspective—not just my technical skills—and my spirit and mind to endure the transition. It was a learning process of grit, resilience, and prayer. I leaned on prayer and community, talking with others who had gone through similar transitions, and I was encouraged by their success.

That was sharpening the right weapons. It was learning to handle the weight of new responsibility, not just by increasing knowledge, but by deepening faith and seeking God's direction. I saw the value of emotional readiness—being calm and centered amid change. This is why sharpening your spiritual ear is so important. It's not just about being prepared physically or intellectually; it's about being fortified spiritually to handle the challenges ahead.

In the second chapter of Acts, Peter finally gets it. He speaks up on behalf of the people filled with the Holy Spirit, declaring the words that the prophet Joel spoke to clarify the moment for those who were confused. His response mirrored his growth. He didn't pull his sword out of its sheath because of the response of the people. This time, he was in tune with the Father, and he responded with grace, love, truth, and conviction. To define Peter's behavior even more clearly, he never drew the sword again. He learned to lean in, trust God, and rely on the process that was tailor-made for his growth.

On the contrary, as we transition from the glorious maturity we witnessed while peeking into the life of Peter, I want to highlight an entirely different scenario. In Genesis 4, a murder occurred from anger. Cain killed Abel. Genesis 4:8 (AMP) says, *"Cain talked with Abel his brother [about what God had said]. And when they were [alone, working] in the field, Cain attacked Abel his brother and killed him."*

Let's take a moment and define murder so that we can extrapolate more meaning from this text. Murder is the premeditated act of killing another human being. Although murder is an extreme case, in many ways, we destroy our circle because of something that we're dealing with internally.

What I love about this scripture in Genesis 4 is that God visits Cain in his sin and encourages him to master it. God sees where Cain is, and He approaches him with a warning about where his unchecked emotions will lead him. Genesis 4:6–7 says, *"Then the LORD said to Cain, 'Why are you angry? And why is your face downcast? If you do what is right, will you not be accepted? But if you do not do what is right, sin is crouching at your door; it desires to have you, but you must rule over it.'"*

God does a random visit to Cain's house, and He notices that it's a mess! Has God ever shown up randomly at your house and discovered how messy it is? You know, we like to tidy up before we have visitors, but God has a way of showing up unannounced in the middle of our breakdown, emotional fit, and moment of rage to have a conversation with us. This is exactly what He does with Cain. As a Father, God visits us to give us an opportunity to consider our ways as He does here in the scripture with Cain.

It's easy to look from the outside, peeking into somebody else's window, determining a solution for their problem, but when the challenge knocks on your door and you are in the middle of your own crisis, perspectives change. I dare not take this moment to judge Cain for how he mistreated his brother, but I would like to talk about what I have observed in scripture. I believe that there are some spiritual moves we can make in our lives so that we don't find ourselves succumbing to the same behavior that Cain fell prey to.

I'm always tickled when I hear people talk about individuals in the Bible. We have a lot of suggestions about what they should've done, how they should've responded, and how they should've believed. We build our own scenarios as we consider how we could've done it better. I'm amazed at how well many of the people in the Bible performed, having substantially fewer resources than we possess in this current era. I think of Job, who had one of the deepest relationships with God that any man could have, and yet he didn't have a Bible, a book, a manuscript, the Pauline epistles, a devotional, a self-help book, or the words of wisdom from spiritual leaders that we so easily take for granted. Job lost everything, yet he was so emotionally disciplined that, rather than cursing God, he fell to his knees and worshiped.

So, I approach this text regarding Cain and Abel with

humility, respect, and a reverential fear of God. One of Cain's mistakes was looking externally rather than internally. I just wonder what Cain's response would've been had there been no conversation with his brother, Abel, about his offering to God. What if God had never accepted Abel's sacrifice? Would Cain have stewed with the same level of anger? What if Cain's offering had been isolated from anyone else's? I wonder if his response would've been the same. I believe our emotions are like the twists and turns of a roller coaster—up and down, around and over—when we subject them to the results of others' success or the lack thereof. Be careful that your emotions don't fluctuate like the stock market based on what's happening with those you are connected to. You must acquire an internal thermostat that regulates your emotional aptitude by your own growth, value, boss moves, progression, and moments of advancement.

I remember when I was working in education. I watched many of my peers go on to be promoted from assistant principal to principal, and I found myself in this place where I had to regulate my emotions and not become bitter because I wasn't chosen. I would be in rooms filled with hundreds of people, watching them be celebrated, and I had to take intentional moments not to allow their success to be a dagger in my heart. It wasn't always easy, but I had to understand that there was something that God was doing in me, just as He was doing in them. It simply wasn't my time.

I learned to swallow my pride and genuinely celebrate them. I made sure my congratulations were authentic, and to my surprise, many of them would share with me how much potential they saw in me to be at that same level. Eventually, I did get the opportunity to step into that role as a summer school principal. It was my chance to demonstrate my skills—putting together schedules, running meetings with teachers, conducting walkthroughs, and ensuring that the school ran smoothly. That experience validated my level of leadership. Although it was a lighter version of principalship, it highlighted my capability to operate at that high level of leadership. It was a reminder that God's timing is perfect, and when it was right, He allowed me to walk in that space without bitterness or regret.

I think of two good-looking gentlemen standing before a beautiful young lady. Both are eager to ask her to the senior prom. Both are vying for her attention. She will only go with one of them. If she picks the young man on the basketball team, will the gentleman on the football team be able to handle the rejection? Why is it that we must spend so much time crafting our choices to cater to the emotions of someone who cannot handle rejection? It causes a conundrum for the young lady, and she has the propensity to get stuck in making a choice for fear of offending the gentleman not chosen. Don't get stuck! The thing I love about God is that He was extremely transparent with both Cain and Abel. God didn't get stuck at the table of decision-making. Based upon His instructions, He either accepted or rejected their offering.

A lesson for you: Stop spending so much time trying to craft an answer that caters to those who cannot handle your choice. It is not your responsibility to pick someone up off the floor because they cannot contain themselves emotionally. After all, you said no. Be delivered from the need to serve everyone in your life a five-course meal on a gold plate to preserve their feelings.

Discover and sustain the people in your life who have the emotional fortitude to handle your response. Anyone unable to digest your honesty shouldn't have a seat at the table with you.

I learned this lesson early as an aspiring musician. I was surrounded by many incredibly talented people. Some of their skills were so sharp that it would make the hair on your arm stand up. But I had to be careful not to connect with certain groups because, while their talent was undeniable, what came with it was a lot of negative nuances—things that were neither integral nor righteous. I had to make a choice: compromise my character for the sake of leveling up my skills or remain true to who I was. Even as a teenager, I sensed God helping me make good decisions and be mindful of the company I kept.

Later, I would discover that in His timing, God would connect me with people who had both great skill and strong integrity. People who loved God and genuinely wanted to see others succeed. I learned that sometimes it's not about rushing to be surrounded by greatness if that greatness is tainted. God will provide the right people, at the right time, and when He does, there's no compromise necessary. I'm sorry to be so blunt, but I know what it is to spend so many moments of your life trying to appease people who will walk away anyway because emotionally, they cannot handle who you are and who you are becoming.

Lord, I pray that you would put us in the path of people who can handle us and who have the emotional fortitude to be able to walk with us even when we say no. Thank you, Father, in Jesus's name, amen.

I felt it necessary to say that prayer because, in the next phase of your life, you must only befriend those who are emotionally ready. You don't have time to babysit. You don't have time to cuddle. Emotional readiness is what you need.

God says sin is crouching at the door of Cain's heart, trying to get in. God describes sin as active and engaging. At Cain's door, sin makes its lair. God was telling Cain to be aware that sin was resting quietly at his heart's door. Lord, I pray that we will be more patient than sin. Lord, I pray that we have the strength to resist the devil so that he may flee.

Cain did more external gazing than internal searching. Take a moment and go into those uncharted spaces and muster up enough strength to be honest with where you are. You may not have killed someone physically, but how many times have you harmed someone because of your inability to deal with your intrinsically raging storm? Regarding those around you whose blessings and success are undeniable, you never once said a word, but your mind continued to create random stories of how they could fail. You dream of their demise. You hope that, at some point, God will reject what they have offered. You must understand that God rejecting their offer does not deal with the sin that lies within your thoughts. At your door, sin makes its lair. You must fight the proposal to harm your brother because of your current rejection.

The cure to contending with that dark place is to discover that God truly loves you as a father loves his son. I love that God came to see Cain to address his sin and anger and warn him of what his future would look like if he did not change his mind. It shows a characteristic of God that has lingered throughout the ages—that God's grace and His mercy are always available.

What an inopportune time for God to show up while Cain was throwing chairs, breaking windows, cursing out the neighbors, and raging beyond control. In the middle of the chaos, He steps in to have a conversation with him. Oh, how powerful is God's presence, His grace, and His mercy toward us. If we would just open ourselves up to receive it. What if Cain had received God's grace rather than letting rage undo who the Father created him to be? What if Cain would have embraced the transparency and honesty that was provided to him? One of the most challenging areas for humanity is to accept the constructive, honest, and naked truth that is provided to us by our circle. Maybe it's God showing up while you are at your worst, giving you an opportunity to make a better decision.

God is accessible. God's arms were open to Cain. I think of the prodigal son who shows up after living a truly wildlife. He shows up at his father's house, and before he can even step fully on the premises, his father sees him and runs to him. Don't miss the moments when God runs to you. Don't miss the moment when God stands on the edge of time waiting for you to decide to change your heart and your mind about where you are.

I want to end this chapter by prompting you to do something important before we move on. You must forgive yourself for what has transpired in your life because of your lack of emotional regulation. There are parts of you that continue to beat yourself up. You say, "If I would have kept my mouth shut…If I would've stayed silent…If I hadn't opened my mouth at that restaurant…If I had continued to walk to my car rather than turn around and say what I said…things would have been different."

One hard truth coming up! What we cannot do is change the past, but what we can do is find a place within ourselves where there is peace and thankfulness for another opportunity to improve who we are. Just like Cain would never have been able to get his brother back, there may be some things that are permanently lost based on your decisions. But it does not mean that you must continue to fall prey to condemnation, guilt, and shame. Today is your day to forgive yourself! Today is your day to look in the mirror and say, "I am not who I used to be." Today is your day to decide to make a U-turn and embrace the grace and mercy that has endured. That grace and mercy are still available to you! Make a conscious decision to realign yourself with God's purpose and will for your life. And who knows? Maybe there will be a redemption story birthed out of those moments in your life when you were out of control. The biggest decision to make is to give yourself the grace that God provides for those of us who miss the mark.

Just a friendly reminder, you are not the atrocious decision you made. Stop the bleeding in your life. Stop labeling yourself by your mishap. You are not what you did, and you are not what happened to you. You may have made a poor decision, but you are not defined by it. You are not the thing that has plagued you for so long. Free yourself, liberate yourself, and find a place of serenity. Declare who you are based on what God's word has said about you. Never define yourself by your darkest times. That is an insult to God who took His time when He created you. There is no other human being on Earth like you. Even identical twins have different fingerprints. I'll repeat what I said earlier: You are fearfully and wonderfully made by God.

BALANCE BUILDER · · · · · · · · · · · · · · · · · · ·

Being emotionally ready means responding with wisdom, not impulse. It's about staying anchored in God's peace even when chaos hits. Balance shows up when your emotions are guided, not suppressed. Choose readiness over reaction—it shapes your future.

Before life gets loud, take a moment to quiet your soul. These questions will help you build the inner strength necessary to respond with grace, focus, and maturity—especially under pressure.

1. What past or present comparisons have made me question my value?

2. How do I typically react when others succeed in areas I'm still waiting on?

3. What spiritual or emotional weapons do I need to sharpen in this season?

4. How has God revealed areas where I need more emotional discipline?

5. What would it look like to embrace God's grace for me and walk in emotional maturity today?

CHAPTER 3

PRESERVATION OF INTEGRITY

. . . .

I'm what you call a church boy. My mom danced and praised God while I was in the womb. She often prayed because of the number of miscarriages she had before my arrival. Although she suffered so much loss, hurt, and pain, she still found a place to trust God and preserve her expectation for something great to happen in her life. I was born out of her tenacity, her ability to keep it together, her commitment to prayer, and her resilience that navigated her to a miracle.

Juxtaposed with my mom was my father, praying and hoping that I wouldn't be the victim of a miscarriage. My dad tells me a story of when he was in the church praying for my safe arrival. He said that God spoke to him and said I would live. God would share some important information about me with my dad that he would hold on to dearly. Later, in my adulthood, my father finally shared with me the sentiments that he received from God. Both of my parents, on separate occasions, had encounters with God on my behalf—speaking of how He would use me and how I would minister to the world in various ways.

Here's my point. In life, we all have a journey that may start rocky. Unfortunately, some of us start life's journey with loss beyond what we feel that we can handle. Some of us have experienced high levels of betrayal that, for some time, caused bitterness. These are moments—just like my mom and my dad experienced—where you must lean on God and trust Him. When life gives you lemons, find some sugar and water to make lemonade.

Can you hold on to the essence of who you are in the toughest of times? Those moments are simply a test of your faith. Mary and Joseph, before the birth of Jesus, had to preserve and protect the information afforded them by the angel. They had to trust God's direction. For God's plan of salvation for mankind to work, He had to be strategic, and He had to find people who, no matter what, could stay focused and allow Him to guide them. What you are carrying will only come to fruition if you stay focused.

This chapter is going to focus on keeping it together in times when life is not easy. In moments of attack, you will not drop your integrity. You will acknowledge God, trust Him, and know that He will cover and protect you through it all.

David was the least likely, in his family, to succeed. He was the last on his father's list to be called when Samuel came to the house of Jesse to anoint the next king. David was called to do tasks that didn't show the best angles of who he was. Yet, God had plans to anoint him to be the next king. David had to discover how to hold on to his integrity while living in a world that forgot that he existed. David was a shepherd who God had called to be a king. David took his job as a shepherd seriously. Little did David know that his shepherding was a training ground for his position as a king.

This reminds me of Stephen Curry's journey from high school to college. Much like David tending sheep in the fields, Curry was largely overlooked during his early years. Major college programs didn't see his potential. Scouts doubted his size, his shooting style, and his ability to compete at the highest level. He wasn't recruited by the powerhouse schools. But despite being overlooked, he remained faithful to the process. He committed to Davidson College—a small school not known for its basketball dominance. Curry took that opportunity and shined, leading Davidson to unexpected victories and proving every scout and critic wrong. His time at Davidson was his training ground, much like David's time in the field. He sharpened his skills, perfected his craft, and eventually became one of the most transformative players in NBA history. What was unseen by the masses was always visible to God, just as David was anointed even before he was acknowledged. Both stories reveal that it is not about the stage you are on; it is about the faithfulness you have while you are there.

David's brothers were envious of him, and they criticized him quite often. Criticism from the outside has a sting, but it doesn't harm you as much as the lack of support that you receive from people you expect to be in your corner, no matter what.

I remember when I moved from my hometown of Nacogdoches where I was serving at my dad's ministry in Diboll, Texas. There were challenges in that transition as to why I would leave my father's ministry and move to Dallas, Texas. The Lord was leading me to Dallas, and that was difficult for some people to digest. I experienced pushback as I prepared to move. Some of the people I expected to support me during that transition were not present, and I had to keep moving forward. Many did support me, but some disappointingly didn't. I knew I was affected by it when, near the end of my time there, some members of my father's church threw my wife, my kids, and me a going-away party. It was beautiful.

When I stood to present and say thank you, I broke down emotionally. Many people didn't know how hard it was for me to make that move. I was following God, and yet I was scared. I had my own questions. I stood there, ready to speak, but I lost my words and just got really emotional. It was at that moment that I realized the weight I had been carrying. But God brought me and my family through that challenging transition. It was proof to me that sometimes you must trust the call, even when the support you expect is not fully there. But because David knew who he was and who his God was, he didn't fall prey to the negative expressions. Also, I believe that his brothers were envious of David's confidence and courage amid adversity.

When people are unsure of themselves, who you are reveals something in them. They come off as envious of you; in reality, they are disappointed with what they see in themselves in contrast to you. Let's take a different approach when people in our circle start attacking us. Let's look at their negative response and convert it into energy. It is a compliment to the strength and courage you possess. Look at all the compliments you've received for such a long time.

David came up against adversity from his family and the Israelites' foe, Goliath. David was fighting a close enemy and hearing the verbal threats of Goliath against the Israelite army.

This reminds me of a time when I had to outlive lies and manipulation that were happening around me to the people in my circle. It was a Goliath-sized task because it was happening in the place that I loved and served the most—the church. I discovered that trying to handle this challenge in my flesh was insurmountable. I had to pray, trust God, and believe that the people who were connected to me knew me better than what I was being accused of. I couldn't walk in pride and think I was above accusation—as they did the same with Jesus. He was graceful through every moment. I confess it was hard, but over time, people began to see the truth. I just needed to keep my composure and not lose it because of the injustice.

At one point, I even apologized when I knew I wasn't wrong. There were moments when I felt unprotected by people who I thought would have my back, but I didn't give up. I stayed prayerful and trusted that God would reveal the truth. Just as David faced Goliath, I had to stand amid accusations and lies and remain steadfast. God showed me that sometimes, the biggest fight isn't with your hands; it's with your heart and your integrity. I realized that overcoming false accusations wasn't about proving my point but outliving the lies with truth and grace. There will be rooms you enter where it will be challenging to determine who truly is your enemy but keep showing up. No matter what, keep showing up. Don't let anyone's internal affairs stop you from becoming great. Remember, your greatness reveals an area in those connected to you that they must personally contend with. It's not your problem! You must find balance within yourself in environments where people are coming against you just because you're advancing.

There is one last portion of scripture that I want to address between David and King Saul. There is a pivot in how King Saul sees David upon hearing of his success with Goliath. Your success is going to breed enemies of all sorts in your life. You must be ready for this. King Saul, the king of Israel, overhears the people singing a song after David kills Goliath. The music that reverberates throughout the camp is, *"King Saul has killed his thousands and David his tens of thousands."*

Upon hearing this, King Saul becomes an enemy of David. Just as David's brothers attacked him, David experienced an attack from the highest level of leadership. David's success revealed the king's inadequacies.

Consequently, David had to learn how to dodge spears that were coming forcefully his way for his demise. You may need to stand up and practice this physically and see it as a move you must make mentally, spiritually, and emotionally.

This reminds me of a moment in my leadership where I had to dodge some "spears" that were thrown my way. I gave a directive to someone I'll call James. I laid out instructions, but James went against them, causing a huge conundrum. I remember doing my best to diffuse the situation, only to find out that the emotional explosion took place anyway. Why? Because James didn't listen. Exactly what I told him would happen, happened. And you know what the kicker is? Because James undermined my directive, I had to pick up the broken pieces. I had to do damage control. As the leader, it was my responsibility to be the person who cleaned it up. And I did just that.

I refused to let James' decision burn up and consume what I was building as a leader. I didn't lose heart. We were able to make it through that challenge. I won't say that James is completely on the straight and narrow, but I realized something powerful: how can you truly see who you are without a James in your life? That experience showed me that sometimes God will place people in your circle who challenge you—not to destroy you, but to sharpen you. It's how you respond that determines whether you grow or get consumed by the chaos. Being balanced is about learning how to continue to serve, be a light, create your community, build your business, raise your children, manage people on your job, and pay tribute to society in a positive way while being flexible and agile because of the weapons that are being thrown at you. Resist the urge to fight back! Mahatma Gandhi says, "First they ignore you, then they laugh at you, then they fight you, then you win!"

Hang on long enough to win. Trouble will not last always. Your ability to have a matrix-like move in your life where you can bend, pivot, turn, and be on high alert for attacks is necessary. If you want to do well and contribute at a high level in your community, then you must remind yourself that your success will give birth to new enemies. If you are willing to live a life with success and unbridled enemies, you'll do well in life. It is inevitable for you to build something great and not have enemies. Can you balance your advancement and adversity simultaneously? Side note: Your adversity has been feeding and giving strength to your advancement this entire time. You don't get stronger in the gym without resistance. Resistance is the tool that will aid you in becoming your best self if you can stay focused. Perspective is everything.

I want to give you a few practical moves that will assist you in being successful and finding balance when your enemies are trying to tip the scales. You must take time to remind yourself of your why. If you need to write it down or tattoo it on your arm—whatever is necessary—you must continually remind yourself of why you are standing up in a room full of thousands of people, why you are giving out those meals to those who are hungry, or why you are showing up for people who are inundated with fear. Remind yourself of why you minister, why you serve, why you are raising your family, and why you are continuing to build those relationships. Your "why" will be the fuel you need to keep going amid testing moments.

Every week, my "why" is what drives me to continue pastoring, despite the many challenges. I must say that it is the greatest opportunity of my life! Intersection Church will be three years old on July 17, 2025. Every Sunday, we set up, worship, and break down. Rinse and repeat. Rain, sleet, snow, heat, and strong winds—we have weathered every storm. Starting from the ground up can be daunting when you drive and see churches with filled parking lots on Sunday mornings. But, no matter what, I have desired to give every person who shows up an opportunity to experience God.

Just recently, I had a gentleman named David who came to my church. David was a first-time guest, and he was concerned about the small crowd. But by the end of the service, he walked up to me with tears in his eyes and said, "I was worried about people being here, but God is here."

There is my why! Every week I show up, let God do what He does, and hope that someone can detect that He is with us. My why as a pastor is for people to have the experience that David highlighted because God is the one who makes the difference. Otherwise, we are a church with an empty shell, but when God shows up, we experience increase, strength, peace, and unspeakable joy. In his book *Start with Why*, Simon Sinek says, "Working hard for something we do not care about is called stress; working hard for something we love is called passion."

REMIND YOURSELF OF PAST SUCCESSES

Secondly, you must remind yourself of past successes. You balance out your life when you can reflect on the achievements that led to your current place in life. Remember how you got here? There is a reason why you are where you are. Reminding yourself of the steps that got you to your present—good work ethic, tenacity, and resilience—is necessary because the very same principles that brought you this far will also elevate you to the next level. Hold on to your grit!

If it's not broken, don't fix it. Your success is predicated upon your tools and experiences. Some of us wonder why we struggle with progress. It may be because we're trying to use tools not designed for us. When David went to fight Goliath, he had to reject the king's armor and the king's weapons. David went with what he knew worked. He didn't get distracted by the grandeur of Saul's armor—he trusted in what God had graced him with. I've heard Bishop T.D. Jakes say on several occasions, "It will work if you work it!"

Don't be intimidated by other people's shiny tools. What God has placed in your hands is more than enough to move forward. Reflect on your past victories and the strategies that led you there. Think back to moments when you triumphed against all odds and remind yourself of the mindset you had during that season. The same grace that carried you through those moments is still with you now.

SPEND TIME IN PRAYER AND MEDITATION

Lastly, ensure you continue to spend time in prayer and meditation. There are strategies on this Earth that are necessary for your continuance. You need heavenly help. Your ability to remain unstoppable lies in the tools you are using and the deep relationship you are building with God. These elements make you resilient. These elements will help you stay balanced when you are challenged beyond what you believe you can handle.

Prayer and meditation are not merely rituals; they are lifelines. When you spend time in the presence of God, you are sharpening your spirit, clarifying your vision, and fortifying your heart against the challenges that arise. Prayer is where you align your thoughts with His thoughts. Meditation is where you allow His Word to marinate in your spirit, giving you the strength to withstand the storms of life.

Think of David as he prepared for battle, not just against Goliath, but throughout his life. His time tending sheep wasn't wasted time; it was preparation. His moments alone in worship and prayer built in him a resilience that would serve him well when the stakes were high. In the same way, your time spent alone with God is not wasted. It is the secret ingredient to your strength.

BALANCE BUILDER · · · · · · · · · · · · · · · · · ·

Integrity is your anchor when everything around you shifts. It's not just about who sees you but who you are when no one's looking. Staying true to your values preserves peace and builds lasting character. Let your integrity be louder than your circumstances.

Integrity is tested most during difficult seasons. These questions will help you examine your ability to stay grounded in who you are, even when you're overlooked, misunderstood, or under attack.

1. When have I felt overlooked or misunderstood, and how did I respond?

2. In what areas of my life is God calling me to preserve my integrity despite opposition?

3. How do I typically handle criticism or lack of support from those I expect to be in my corner?

4. Who or what reminds me of my "why" when I feel like giving up?

5. What practical steps can I take to remain faithful, focused, and balanced in the face of resistance?

CHAPTER 4

HEALING FROM IDENTITY CRISIS

· · · · · · · · · · ·

Anybody who has spent any time with me knows that I love *The Matrix* series. Neo is one of my favorite characters because we get an opportunity to peer into his life as he begins to discover who he truly is. It's interesting because, as he lived in the present, it was almost as if his future haunted him. He couldn't explain it, but something was calling him to a level of greatness that was beyond his present circumstances. In this chapter, I want to focus on you finding the greatness that is within. I want to break down the process of finding that greatness because so often we look outward. We look beyond our borders to try to find what was brilliantly placed within us before the foundations of the world. It's only been lying dormant for a season, waiting for us to learn how to become excavators of our hidden treasure.

Is it possible to be actively doing something that you don't believe you can do? When I started learning to ride a bike, I remember my cousins giving me the best training. They would stand behind me, give me a good start, and talk to me as I steered the bike and pedaled. I could hear my cousin's voice close behind me, holding me up and helping me stay balanced.

I remember that there was a time when I was riding the bike, unbeknownst to me, my cousin had released his grip, and I was doing it on my own. I was riding the bike independently, and I had no idea. The moment I discovered that no one was guiding me, I got anxious, lost balance, and ended up running into the rear bumper of one of the neighbors' cars. I must mention that my cousin was much taller than me, and upon hitting the rear bumper of the car, my feet did not land on the ground. I landed on the bar between the seat and the handles. It was not a pleasant experience. Although I had to contend with the pain of the landing, I discovered that I could ride a bike. I was doing something that I thought I could not do by myself. Anxiety crept in upon discovering that I was alone.

Knowledge can be a problem! I was riding just fine until I became aware that no one was guiding me. Is it possible that what you know can be an impediment blocking the highest level of your potential? Philippians 4:6–7 says, *"Be anxious for nothing, but in everything by prayer and supplication, with thanksgiving, let your requests be made known to God; and the peace of God, which surpasses all understanding, will guard your hearts and minds through Christ Jesus."*

Walk through this chapter allowing your heart to be guarded by God's heavenly peace. Choose to not be anxious about who is not with you. Walk in a place of discovery of what you can accomplish, who you can become, and what God has placed inside of you. There are some great things there. Don't deny yourself the privilege of becoming who God ordained you to be. Do not deny yourself from becoming!

I pray that God will put people around you that will help you to birth who you truly are. I pray that the spiritual midwives that are assigned to you will be revealed.

For a couple of years, I went to the University of Houston before transferring to Stephen F. Austin State University in my hometown of Nacogdoches, TX. At the University of Houston, I met two guys named Tai and Chris. Little did I know that God had strategically planned that moment.

I remember one moment when Tai and Chris were standing on one side of my dorm room as I stood on the other. They just stared at me and slightly chuckled. It wasn't a condescending chuckle; they were entertained by me not knowing who I truly was and what God would do through me as we all worked together on the college campus to minister to young adults. I would go on to work closely with Chris and Tai, where hundreds of young adults would be inspired, coached, and uplifted by the teaching of God's word. I was a part of that movement. I had no idea that I was an answer to a prayer for them. All the while, they saw it as I stumbled around in my head to become what they could see. How could they see it and I not see it? How do other people see in you what you don't see in yourself? I've discovered that those individuals are simply called by God to help, guide, and aid you in discovering who He called you to be.

In the Bible, Jeremiah was a young prophet, and God called him to speak to the people on His behalf. God speaks to Jeremiah and tells him that he's going to be a prophet to the nations. Jeremiah says, *"Ah, Lord God! Behold, I cannot speak, for I am a youth."*

It took some guts for Jeremiah to say this to God the Father rather than just accepting what He said as truth. I believe it was the absurdity of the comment that God made that made Jeremiah respond the way that he did. Jeremiah was very astute to those who were prophets among him, and he didn't believe that he fit the bill. God, however, did not allow Jeremiah to linger in his disbelief. He told him, *"Do not say, 'I am a youth,'"* because the Lord would put the words in his mouth.

Could it be that your own words have chained you to your current situation, not allowing you to be free to become who you truly are? The power of life and death is in the tongue. Many times, we are saying who we are based upon how we see ourselves, but we've not had a conversation with God. It is that conversation with God that, if you allow it, will transform your life. God knows that this conversation with Jeremiah is necessary before using him to minister to the children of Israel. After all, he could not be fully operational until he first understood who he was.

Your real issue is not performance; it is identity. You constantly fight with who God is saying that you are. I want to encourage you today to stop fighting with God. Just accept it as truth. It's like my story of riding a bike and being in sole control of it; I had no idea. I was charting new territory unaware.

Change your internal conversations. Have you been contradicting what God is saying about you? It is time for your tongue to be delivered from its erroneous behavior. No one can do this for you. You must make a conscious decision to change what you say about yourself. If you notice, Jeremiah was stating a fact. But his facts about himself were contradictory to the truth that God was speaking over him. Be careful not to fall prey to what is fact in your life because truth will always trump fact. It is factual that Jeremiah was young, but the truth declared him to be a prophet. Jeremiah's expression of fact— "I am young"—revealed limitations. God's word— "You are a prophet"—opened the door to a world of impossibilities. All things are possible to them that believe! There is a song that says, "Only believe, only believe, all things are possible if you only believe."

Jeremiah had to decide to believe in what God said. You will have to decide to believe what God has said about you. Don't question it. Just believe it. Just walk in it. Just become what God has declared over your life. If you notice in scripture, there was not a lot of time spent on Jeremiah trying to lean into what God said about him. The urgency of the message that God called him to speak required him to trust God and walk in it.

Your purpose birthed out of God's plan for your life comes with a level of urgency. I don't know what it is that God has called you to do, but I can tell you that it is necessary for you to be able to switch gears quickly and stay focused on what He's calling you to. You must know, trust, and believe.

MONITOR WHAT YOU SAY AND HEAR

After monitoring what you say, you must then put yourself in the place to listen closely to God's instructions for your life. Your identity is locked up in what you say and what you hear. If you are struggling with seeing yourself as God sees you, the first thing that you should check is what you are saying and what you are hearing. This may mean that you must check your circle of influence. You must go back and check what's entering through your ear gate. Discover what it is that you are hearing and what you are saying that is causing there to be this place in you that struggles with acknowledging who you truly are.

So, what if no one has ever done it before? Don't let your identity crisis stop you from being great. No one else can stop you. Stop trying to rationalize and qualify yourself—or disqualify yourself—for that matter. Just walk in the confidence of God's word. Tasha Cobbs has a song that says I have confidence. You may need to check that song out. Just play the song repeatedly until you get it. You don't have a lot of time. We are all running out of time, and we must come into agreement with what God has said about us.

Consider what God said to Adam and Eve in the garden. God asked them, "Who told you that you were naked? Have you eaten from the tree of which I commanded you that you should not eat?"

We echo the sentiments of what we see rather than remembering what God has said. What did He say to you? In your dreams, what did God say to you? Through a vision, what did the Lord say about you? As you were reading His word, what do you remember Him saying? That word while you were in church that resonated so deeply with you that you got emotional—can you remember what the Lord was speaking to you? Let it reign true over everything else. I have a place on my mirror where I've written reminders down. When I'm brushing my teeth or washing my face, I see them and am reminded of my purpose. Find a way to remind yourself of where you're going.

Before we transitioned to Dallas—a new area, new venture, new experiences—we were in my hometown. I spoke to my dad, who was the pastor of the church that I served, a year prior to leaving about my transition. Six months before moving, we turned one of our rooms into a storage unit. I was traveling back and forth from Dallas—a three-and-a-half to four-hour journey—to attend interviews and job fairs. It was bananas. I was still serving at my father's church and traveling when I could to secure a job for the family.

People would come to the house and see the boxes. They would see us packing, and they would ask the question that I dreaded so often. They would ask me about my progression in locking down a place to stay, a job, or an area. I would talk about the interviews and the prospective locations, but for a long time, I could never share substantiated evidence that gave anyone confidence that this transition was going to be smooth. So, every day, although I thought it was a good idea, the boxes in that room started psychologically mocking me. It was like: You got boxes packed, but you don't have a job.

I had to trust God's word. I had to trust what He said to

me six months ago. You won't believe it, but we were in the last month before moving when I got a call to sign my contract with a school district. I had bags packed and boxes stacked, and we had locked down a nice, economically friendly apartment, but I still struggled to lock down the job. A few weeks before leaving, it all worked out. Out of the 365 days of a year, God revealed my place of employment around the 351st day.

You must continually remind yourself of God's promises and His direction when you are in the toughest places in your life. Let God's word that He spoke to you months ago feed you in your present. Let trust be the bridge over troubled waters, and God will do exactly what He said He would do. It has been said that He may not come when you want Him, but He will be there right on time.

I want to share something with you: God doesn't live in time. He is eternal. We are waiting for a manifestation of something that has already been established. It was established at the moment that you grabbed ahold of what God said. Manifestation is marked by time. But it was done when God said it. Just like the Earth had to catch up with what God declared in eternity, so will your life catch up with what God declared in eternity. When our feet landed in Dallas, we had everything we needed for the next level of work that God called us to.

Recently, I was being guided in an area where I did not have a lot of expertise. The person helping me had the experience, skill, and knowledge. We will call this individual Amy. Amy was walking me through the steps to accomplish the task, and she was so confident in what she knew. Because I didn't know what I was doing, I followed suit. As she walked me through the process, something clicked in me, and I had an idea. I asked Amy if that would be the appropriate next route to go to accomplish the task. Amy said, "No, you shouldn't do that."

Well, I reached out to another colleague about solving this problem and handling the task. James mentioned the same idea I had brought up to Amy, and she dismissed it. I walked through the steps with Amy, and she said, "Okay, all done! You are good now."

I then decided to attempt the idea that I had thought of and that James mentioned to me. What do you know—my idea worked! For a moment, I was prideful. I wanted to tell Amy that my idea, which she shut down, worked. But out of humility, I kept my thoughts to myself. I wondered where that idea came from. How did I know that? I believe that just because people have confidence doesn't mean that they are accurate. There are times when confidence can be misinterpreted as the right way. It is possible to go confidently in the wrong direction. But that stirring deep within knew that there was a better way. You must tap into those places as they will rescue you from following the wrong voice.

I repeat—just because a voice is confident doesn't mean that it should have jurisdiction in your life. Be careful what you allow into your ear and who you allow to guide you. This will deter you from the disappointment of collateral damage because you didn't follow your instincts.

I was sitting at my desk in la-la land. I was stressed. It seemed like the more I accomplished, the more work appeared in my life.

I had several projects going, I was working, I was taking care of the family, I was handling ministry, and I was being stretched beyond my limits. In a moment of reflection, I just stopped. I rested my chin on my hands, and I clamped together almost in a posture of prayer. As I took a moment to reflect and try to find sense in the craziness, I looked to my left. There was my keyboard, set up, powered up, and the Lord prompted me to sit at the keyboard and just play.

I was so stressed out. I started to sing, "Ohhhhh tell me, who can, stand before us, when we, call on, that great name, Jesus, Jesus, precious, Jesus, we have the victory!"

At one moment I just sustained the keys on the keyboard, and the last chord I played just dwelled and filled the room. It was a piano with strings, and as that last chord lingered in the room, I started to feel relief. My circumstances didn't change, but I began to feel a shift in my thoughts. My heart started to lift, and my outlook on life began to change. God began to lift me out of the trenches of despair. It was that moment of worship that operated like wings beneath me and took me up beyond my problems.

God revealed to me the true power of obedience, guidance, praise, and worship in that moment. I had to be obedient, trust God, and move to the keyboard. Who would've thought with no one in the room that just a moment in God's presence would change everything? We talk about God a lot, but we don't talk to Him as much. We don't adore Him as much as we talk at Him. We ask for more than we give. At that moment, I didn't have anything else to give. All I had was an alabaster box full of oils to anoint Jesus.

You may not have anything but pull out your alabaster box like Mary did to anoint Jesus's body. Let Him know that without Him you are nothing. When you find yourself empty, praise until you're full. Praise yourself out of and into. Worship God in spirit and truth and watch the healing that takes place. Mary began to anoint Jesus because she realized who was the most important person in the room. When you are overwhelmed, remember who the most important person in the room is and find yourself in a posture of worship.

My daughter Kaalyn and I had a season where we were going to The Potter's House on Wednesdays. Side note: Most times, we would stop by Chick-fil-A on the way home and enjoy a meal on the run together. I remember there was a Wednesday when my soul was just restless. Bishop Jakes preached a powerful word. It was April 12, 2023, and he was dressed in all white. At the end of the sermon, he had a bucket of water and used it as a symbol of being refreshed and revived. I cannot remember the title of the message, but what I do remember is that word lifting me up. I came in with what felt like a bag of rocks in the pit of my stomach. I was sinking, and by the end of that word, I was light as a feather.

The Bible says that God's word is a lamp unto our feet and a light unto our pathway. On that Wednesday night, my heart was lit up, and I could see a path that was invisible before. The power of God's word changes the makeup of your situation and sets you free. Sometimes you don't even need the title of the message—just the residue of His presence is enough to transform you. I left that service knowing that the power of what you hear can shift your entire perspective. It is crucial to find yourself in the right places where God's word is being spoken because His word changes everything.

What you hear is just as critical as what you say. Faith comes by hearing the Word of God. If you constantly feed yourself with negativity and doubt, you will inevitably find it hard to believe in your purpose. You are the steward of your ear gate. Be intentional about what you allow to be spoken into your life. Sometimes, it's not just about avoiding negative people; it's about shutting down negative self-talk. For years, I allowed myself to hear voices of doubt and disbelief, even within my mind. I had to intentionally change the narrative.

One of the most transformative practices I began was listening to scripture audibly. Hearing God's promises over and over began to reprogram my thinking. It's the same concept as learning the lyrics to a song. You hear it enough times, and eventually, you know it by heart. If you saturate your hearing with God's promises, eventually, you'll believe them. Make it a priority to protect what enters your ear gate. God is speaking, but if the noise is too loud, you won't hear Him.

BALANCE BUILDER

You are not defined by your wounds or your past. True healing begins when you believe what God says about you. Balance returns when you start accepting who you already are in Him. Your identity is your foundation. Walk in it boldly.

You were created with purpose and power. These questions will help you confront your self-perception, align with God's voice, and overcome the voices internal and external that have tried to define you.

1. Where in my life have I allowed fear, comparison, or anxiety to block me from becoming who God says I am?

2. What beliefs do I have about myself that contradicts God's truth about me?

3. Who are the people God has placed in my life to guide, affirm, or birth what's inside me?

4. How can I practically monitor what I say and what I hear to protect my God-given identity?

5. What spiritual practices help me reconnect with who God says I am, especially when I feel lost, unseen, or overwhelmed?

CHAPTER 5

AN ATTRACTION TO THE IMPOSSIBLE

· · · · · · · · · · · ·

I told my dad at a young age—so young I could hardly reach the pedal—that I could play the drums. Initially, he didn't believe me. Now, you must understand the absurdity of the whole situation. I was so young that the tom-toms towered over me. You could hear the bass, the snare, and the crashing of cymbals, but you would have thought, "There's no one there!" I was too short to play sitting on the seat, so I had to play standing up. You can see why my dad thought it was impossible. He was a musician, and he soon discovered that the music that lived in him also lived in me. What seemed like an impossible task was happening. Have you ever been in a moment where something seemed impossible, yet you were doing it?

When I was young, I was timid. I struggled with expressing myself, and I wasn't sure if anyone was listening. I didn't want to waste my words, especially if I thought they would fall to the ground. I was quiet. I was inconspicuous. I preferred to be in the back of the room, staying unseen. I'm amazed that, as someone so comfortable being behind the scenes, God would call me to be a pastor. Another absurdity, in my opinion. If you had asked me during those years of extreme timidity and anxiety if I would ever be a pastor, I would have laughed myself into a coma. But here I am, walking in impossibilities.

The contradiction for me is that, coupled with my timidity, I always had a high level of inquisitiveness. Some of you can relate to this—you are accustomed to comfort, but you keep dreaming about worlds that seem untouchable.

If I can be honest, what I hate the most is for someone to tell me what I cannot do. I don't lock up or become frustrated to the point of paralysis. Those words become fuel for me to advance and conquer.

I remember being at the basketball court when I was younger, playing with some family members, friends, and this random guy who showed up. We all thought he looked like Michael Jordan. He was tall, mature, and dominant on the court. I remember him ejecting our shots from the goal with ease. This is where I first realized my attraction to impossibilities. No matter how many times he sent my basketball to the other side of the court, I couldn't force myself to stop going toward the goal. Whether it was a layup or a dunk—both impossibilities for me at that time—I wouldn't stop advancing. No matter how many times he slapped my shot out of the air, I couldn't stop moving forward.

The more he blocked my shots, the more resilient and

determined I became. I ignored the embarrassment, the laughter from my friends, and the opinions of anyone watching. I was so determined to outplay this man who had more experience, height, strength, and maturity. I was driven by an attraction to what seemed impossible.

Your next level of work is going to require an attraction to the impossible. Let the crowd laugh and mock you, but don't give up. There is nothing wrong with you. You find yourself pushing and advancing to become someone or achieve something that seems unreachable. But your determination, inquisitiveness, resilience, and need to see what's on the other side will be the driving force that allows you to witness the impossible.

There are lessons I learned from that challenging moment with that random guy on the court—lessons I never would have seen playing with those of similar ability. That moment taught me what was in me. That moment taught me that there is something more in life that extends beyond the natural eye.

Often in my dreams, I find myself soaring through the air, tasting the clouds and feeling the coolness of the wind. I stretch out my arms, measuring my wingspan, or sometimes I close my eyes and simply feel the breeze rush past me. Only to wake up to a world tethered by gravity. I understand that dreams can sometimes be chaotic and unexplainable, but I believe there are moments when we are given glimpses of the impossible to widen our view of ourselves and our God.

I'm grateful for the stunning visuals that movies provide—those larger-than-life superheroes who can leap across buildings and defy the laws of nature. I use those moments to imagine myself breaking past the ordinary, reaching heights unknown. But it's not just about dreaming; it's about breaking free from what has become normal, stretching your mind to consider who you truly are and who you can become.

I believe that a lack of knowledge can limit us from experiencing the best in life. I remember the story of Jesus speaking to a woman at the well in the Bible. He told her, "If you knew who I was, you would be asking me for a drink." That moment speaks to me. It reminds me that part of our challenge in accessing the highest levels of opportunity in life is rooted in not recognizing the possibilities that are wrapped up in the knowledge of God. That's why I urge you to ask questions, be inquisitive, and sharpen your mind by accumulating wisdom.

I pray that you develop an attraction to the impossible. This is crucial for creating balance in areas of your life where you're called to step beyond the boundaries of the familiar and tread into new territory. There must be a part of you that craves the impossible more than the comfort of the present. This desire will motivate you during moments when friends or family may be skeptical or even condescending about your leaps of faith. You must learn to silence the noise of opinions that attempt to drown out your vision.

When I was in education, I wanted to move from being a teacher to becoming an administrator. For over ten years, I worked in a school district in the Dallas-Fort Worth Metroplex. I remember one moment when I shared my desire to pursue an assistant principal role—the typical next step from teaching. The responses I received were far from encouraging. People shared their stories of how long it took for them to advance, and most of them told me not to expect it to happen anytime soon.

These weren't just random people; these were administrators—the very people who had already made it to where I wanted to go. I was stunned to hear such negativity from those who had already traveled the road I was preparing to walk. My heart raced, and I felt discouragement creeping in. Maybe it would be best to just remain a teacher, I thought. If it was going to take three, maybe even five years to get there, was it even worth trying? I had earned my master's degree in educational leadership and felt ready for the next step. But standing there in that circle of doubt, I questioned if I should even fill out the internal application.

But my attraction to the impossible pushed me forward. Despite the voices that told me it wouldn't happen, I went through the grueling interview process. And what do you know? I landed the position on my very first attempt. I'll never forget the looks of surprise on the faces of the same people who told me it would take years. That experience taught me something powerful: you can't let someone else's story write the narrative for your life.

What are you waiting for? Are you hesitating because someone else's journey planted seeds of doubt? Be careful not to adopt the experiences of others as your own. It doesn't mean you won't face rejection, but it does mean that you owe it to yourself to tell your own story—to leap when others are standing still. I secured a promotion against the odds because I refused to let someone else's timeline dictate mine. That experience taught me to make more noise with my actions than the noise of opinions swirling around me. You have the power to define your path. Don't wait for validation. Leap.

I love the story in the Bible of Jesus and Peter. Jesus is walking on water, and at first, the disciples think it's a ghost, but as He gets closer, they realize it is Jesus. Peter sees Jesus. No, Peter really sees Jesus. Along with the other disciples, he is struggling in his mind because of what he is witnessing. I'm not sure if anybody else thought this, but in the scripture, we know for sure that Peter expressed it.

In Matthew 14, Peter asks Jesus a bold question. Peter says, "If it is you, Jesus, that's walking on the sea, allow me to come." Jesus responds simply, "Come." Peter now has a decision to make. He must decide to leave what is normal in his familiar circle and jump off the boat to be in the presence of Jesus. What's intriguing is that Peter didn't ask Jesus if he could walk on water—he only asked to come to Him. Unbeknownst to Peter, his desire to be with Jesus would require him to defy the laws of gravity. Peter walked on water!

Principle: To do the impossible, you must hang out with people who are doing the impossible.

You may have no connection to that level of achievement in your life, but you choose to befriend those who are. You've never seen a million dollars in the bank, but you decide to hang out with millionaires. You've never purchased a car with cash, but you connect with someone who can have a car delivered to their home with a snap of their fingers. You take a leap of faith and propose to someone of a different culture, monetary status, or pedigree. You ask them to mentor you because you have an attraction to the impossible.

It's uncomfortable to do something you've never seen done before. Peter jumps off the boat and walks on water. I can imagine that most of the disciples even considered asking Jesus if they could come. Most people around you won't have the same inclination to ask bold questions or take big risks. That's why your circle is so important. You need to go for more. But you also must be mentally balanced enough to detect those moments when it's time to move. It was a moment that everyone else in the boat missed—but not Peter.

Make sure you are sensitive to those moments when it's necessary to move so that you can take the leap of faith. You must always be looking for more. You must be hungry and thirsty for something beyond you. God doesn't allow you to see miracles, witness greatness, and observe the impossible just so you can clap from the bleachers. It's your time to jump. Stop waiting for someone else to tell you to leap. Stop sitting on the sidelines discussing where you could go. Stop having conversations about possibility—and just jump.

I studied how people who went skydiving described the experience. Every emotion you can imagine—jumping out of a plane into open space at the mercy of wind and gravity—emerges all at once. Fear, exhilaration, uncertainty, and thrill all collide. I've heard there is a combination of fear and exhilaration that unveils itself during the skydive. Yet, the sense of accomplishment when it's over is often the same. They did something most people would never do.

This chapter is about encouraging you to do things that produce both fear and exhilaration at the same time. I want you to become comfortable with balancing those two feelings that come from acts of faith. You will do what most people say is impossible. You need to develop a "just do it" attitude. Before you finish this chapter, bookmark this page, make a decision, and just do it. Don't think—just do. You've been thinking long enough. You've been weighing your options long enough. It's go-time. It's time to take that leap of faith and make the decision you've been contemplating for so long.

The only reason you haven't moved is because of fear. Fear is not of God. He said He has given us a spirit of love, power, and a sound mind. I'm not telling you to wait for fear to disappear—I'm telling you to do it in the presence of fear. Watch how fear, exhilaration, confidence, courage, and joy all begin to intermingle until fear no longer has a hold on your life. You must learn to do it scared. This is part of the balance in your life. You don't wait for fear to disappear before you take a leap of faith—you do it afraid. The Bible says perfect love drives out fear. When you truly embrace God's love for you and His desire to see you succeed, fear will begin to dissipate.

When my kids were young, I would toss them into the air and catch them. Not once did I ever drop them. You must remember whose hands you are in. God releasing you for a moment should not produce anxiety—it should produce trust. Know that He will always catch you.

Find balance in your life, especially in the areas where you are becoming what you've never been exposed to. Begin by monitoring your circle, confronting your fears, and simply jumping—just doing it. Connect with those who are doing the impossible and anchor yourself with a solid support system.

I want you to look at the word impossible as two words: **I'm possible**. Every time you find yourself saying, "This is impossible," break that word apart and declare, "I'm possible."

If becoming a millionaire seems impossible in your thoughts, shift your perspective. Speak from the mindset of a millionaire and declare, "I'm possible." If building a new business feels unreachable, write out a business plan and stamp it with the words, "I'm possible."

Embody whatever it is that you once believed was impossible and boldly affirm, "I'm possible." Put a picture on your wall of a check for $1,000,000, and on the signature line, write: "I'm possible." If you desire to lose 100 pounds, write down that number boldly at the bottom, and sign it with "I'm possible."

If there is a relationship that has been strained—one that you hold dearly—if it is God's will for your life, it will be restored. But first, write out your vision of that relationship from a healthy perspective. At the bottom, sign it with "I'm possible."

Start signing your life's narratives with this declaration over what you once considered impossible: **I'm possible.**

Life and death are in the power of your tongue. Speak life over yourself, over your children, over your businesses, over your bank account, over your relationships, over your marriage, over your promotion, over your family. And as you speak, keep signing it with: **I'm possible.**

BALANCE BUILDER ····················

When God calls you to the impossible, He also equips you for it. Faith opens doors that logic cannot. Walking in the impossible is not about being fearless but about choosing to move forward despite your fear. Let God stretch your vision and increase your capacity.

This chapter challenges you to confront the limits you've unknowingly accepted. These questions are designed to reignite your faith, silence any doubt, and move you toward bold action.

1. What's one moment in my life when I unknowingly stepped into something I thought was impossible?

2. What fear, voice, or opinion have I allowed to shape my limits?

3. How can I reframe my past discouragements as training for the extraordinary step?

4. Who do I need to surround myself with to encourage my next leap of faith?

5. What is one bold, immediate action I can take today to declare "I'm possible" moving forward?

CHAPTER 6

A YIELDING HEART

. . . .

On July 17, 2022, we opened the doors of Intersection Church in Denton, TX. That moment—establishing Intersection Church—was birthed out of deep prayer with God. I wasn't asking for this. To be honest, I wasn't even that excited about it. In the back of my mind, I kept thinking about how many churches were already established. Building a church from the ground up felt like a saturated decision. There were already so many ministries springing up across the Dallas-Fort Worth Metroplex. I didn't see the point.

I believe I mentioned in another chapter that I covet the back seat. I genuinely have no desire to drive or lead, yet I've been called to do so. I must admit, when I sensed God calling me to start the ministry, I was torn. Around the age of 40, I kept hearing the number 43. I shared with a few people that this number kept appearing—it was persistent and unshakable. Unbeknownst to me, 43 would be the age that the Lord would call me to pastor Intersection Church.

At that time, I was serving at Dayspring Family Church in Irving. I loved it there. Serving under my pastors was fulfilling. But if I'm transparent, launching a ministry would mean a reduction in my salary as I was a musician there. It would require more than just a financial sacrifice; I would need to trust God to fund a ministry that had no space and no people. It had to be God.

As I write this, Intersection Church is two years old, and in three months, we will celebrate our third anniversary. God has been faithful. This journey has not been without its challenges, but it has been worth every moment.

I shared this story at the beginning of this chapter to encourage you as you have your own experiences with God—when He calls you to do something that doesn't make sense. I wrestled with balance—thoughts of inadequacy, concerns about finances, questions of support (or lack thereof), fear of criticism, and the anxiety of the unknown.

I remember that first Sunday, July 17, 2022, our very first service. My pastors showed up to support me, but if I'm honest, that day was a blur. I was so anxious, so nervous, and so incredibly high-strung that I never really got a chance to take a deep breath and truly celebrate the moment. Later, I felt impressed upon—by God—to learn how to settle in and embrace the first.

There is something precious about the first. It's rare, and because of its uniqueness, it is necessary to truly step back, embrace it, and learn from it. Learn from doing something you've never done before.

I said "yes" to what God impressed upon me to do, and I experienced every emotion known to man in the process. Saying "yes" can be depleting—if I'm honest. Relinquishing my will for God's will was challenging. Can you imagine being called to what seemingly looks like nothing? I'm not trying to be disrespectful to the call; I'm just expressing how I felt at that time.

The Lord later explained to me why I needed to start this ministry from the ground up. I remember thinking, "That would have been great information to have at the beginning. But God saw differently."

THE PURPOSE BEHIND THE CALLING

I often wonder why God calls us into these uncomfortable situations. But I realize now that what I consider to be an uncomfortable calling is me walking in God's purpose. His will and His purpose have always been more significant than my feelings of inadequacy.

Simultaneously, as I struggled with saying "yes" to God, I was also putting a pause on His purpose for my life. Understand this: the longer you sustain the space between God's calling and your "yes," the longer you pause His purpose from being fulfilled.

We must realize that the calling is just one part of a greater whole. That whole is God's purpose and His will—it is the driving force behind the call. You were only called because God has a purpose for your life. Something He needs you to do.

And sometimes, delaying your "yes" can be detrimental. Not

just to you but to those who require what God wants to pour out through you. We are all cups—vessels—to be offered up and poured out for the purpose and will of God.

I know you have your aspirations, desires, wants, and inclinations. But understand this: all of those are trumped by God's purpose.

I want to prepare you because this chapter may be one of the most challenging. I believe I'm somewhat qualified to write this chapter because of the number of times I misunderstood what it truly meant to say "yes" to God's will for my life. I absolutely believe in free will—that God provided us with the ability to choose. But the deeper you go into God, you begin to develop a desire where your will intertwines with His. At that level, your will becomes secondary, and His will becomes primary.

This chapter will require you to consider your life choices and question whether you have truly said "yes" to His purpose. One of the most powerful threads throughout Jesus's ministry is that He was always doing the will of His Father. He said that when you see Him, you see the Father because "I am in Him, and He is in me." Jesus's will was so intertwined with His Father's that He could boldly declare, "When you see Me, you see Him."

Can we say the same about our lives? When people see us, do they see the Father?

I remember a time when I answered the phone at the house, and my mother immediately started talking. After a few moments, I realized the conversation wasn't meant for me. I interrupted and said, "Hey Mom, you're actually talking to Tim." She paused and replied, "You sound just like your dad; I thought I was talking to him."

There should come a point when we are so yielded to God's will for our lives that we are indistinguishable from Him.

THE COST OF SAYING "YES"

Can I be honest? I used to be frustrated because saying "yes" to God often meant saying "no" to something else. And if I'm being real, there were times I said "no" to things I wanted to say "yes" to. But because I wanted to please God, I complied.

Someone reading this might think, "That sounds like a miserable way to live." But I've discovered that the benefits of saying "yes" to God completely outweigh the "no" to my subjective desires. I learned that God was always listening and that He knew my desires. Sometimes what I wanted was locked up in my saying "yes" to Him.

The other side of this struggle was my arrogance—thinking that I truly knew what was best for my life. I'm learning now that I've never really known what that is. And if you're honest with yourself, you'll realize that we often think we know the path to greatness, success, and fulfillment. But in the grand scheme of things, the greatest plan ever designed for my life was written by God.

I've had my arrogant moments where I thought I knew better. Those moments always ended with me coming back, humbled and apologetic, like the prodigal son who returned home after squandering his inheritance. When that son came back, his father was there, waiting, watching, and ready to embrace him. That's the God we serve. He's always there.

But we cannot escape the larger question: Should I yield my heart to God's plan for my life?

THE GARDEN OF GETHSEMANE – YIELDING UNDER PRESSURE

Jesus, in the Garden of Gethsemane, had this moment. I can't describe it as beautiful; it's painful to read. It stirs angst and anxiety every time I revisit it. Although I wasn't there at that moment, I can relate to the agony of wanting the moment to be removed. I don't know if you've ever been in a place where you just wanted the weight of it all to go away.

You can see the benefits of pressing through, but at the moment, the weight of your "yes" feels insurmountable. Jesus prayed to the Father, perspiring and leaning in with a request for the cup to be passed from Him. He asked three times for God's purpose to be removed, yet He always ended with, "Nevertheless, Thy will be done."

I can't do justice to that text—the divine collaboration between God the Son and God the Father. But I know this: I can see myself in that moment.

There will be times when you don't feel a single nudge to lean towards God's purpose. But you must find that place within yourself where you can still say, "Nevertheless, Your will be done."

That phrase isn't popular. I live among people—no judgment—who would never yield themselves to that level of submission to God. It takes grit, resilience, and a high level of intestinal fortitude to say "yes" when every part of you wants to say "no."

The agony must have been unbearable for Jesus because He knew the end from the beginning. Yet, in that moment, He still struggled with the weight of surrender. To know the end but still struggle in the middle to say "yes" speaks to the real pain associated with obedience.

THE SEESAW OF SURRENDER

Sometimes, balance in your life when saying "yes" to God looks like imbalance. It's like a seesaw where one end is grounded by a person 100 pounds heavier, while you're flailing on the other side, trying desperately to touch the ground. There are moments when balance means being okay with not being in control.

The humility that develops in you when you learn to be an amazing leader who also follows well is unmatched. God showed me that the level of my ability to follow aligns directly with my capacity to lead.

I think of David, who could have cut off the head of King Saul just as he did with Goliath. Saul was smaller than Goliath, yet David refused to harm him. Despite knowing Saul meant him harm, David honored his position as king. He trusted God's timing.

David was anointed king but never once revealed that to Saul. He continued to respect Saul's office and preserve his life, even when he knew Saul's intentions. That is the power of a yielded heart.

This is the chapter where there is simply one way to get through those difficult moments where you must yield your heart—and that is **trust**.

Trust is your ability to believe in the integrity, the ability, and the character of God. It is having confidence in Him, even when you cannot see a favorable outcome. It's the place where you must allow a space for just trust.

The Bible says, "One plants, another waters, but God grants the increase." When you say "yes" to God, you must trust Him for the increase. You have to believe that His plan and purpose are best, even when you have no empirical data to support it.

We live in a world that thrives off data. Tables, graphs, and spreadsheets fill our days, tracking our progress and measuring our success. Then, you have God, who comes along, takes every single data sheet known to man, rips it up, and simply says, "Follow me."

WHEN DATA DOESN'T APPLY

Know that where the Lord is taking you, data sheets may not apply. If you notice, when Jesus began His ministry, there were no parameters or guides to determine the validity of His words. Jesus would have a conversation with the Father and then speak with His disciples based on that conversation.

He would say things so profound that at times people scratched their heads and questioned if they had made the right choice to follow Him. Many times, when you have a conversation with God and then share that information with others, it's challenging for them to digest. There are no parameters, no origins to trace, just a word from God.

We like to know who said it, when they said it, and how they said it. But when it comes to God and His instructions, there's only one place to meet Him, and that is the place called trust.

MOSES AND THE POWER OF TRUST

When Moses went to Egypt to deliver the children of Israel from the tyrannical grip of the Pharaoh, he simply said, "God said to let My people go, so they could worship Me in the wilderness."

To the Pharaoh, that made no sense. Why would he let go of the people who built his kingdom on their backs? Why would he release his labor force just so they could worship a God he neither respected nor honored?

I can imagine the Pharaoh looking at Moses with a side-eye, thinking, "The audacity of you." This type of approach to freeing the Israelites required Moses to **trust God**. All he had to work with was a word. And yet, from that single word, something miraculous was birthed because Moses yielded his will to God's.

THE SEESAW OF TRUST AND BALANCE

This is where many of us start to feel it's not fair. This is the chapter where some might argue, "I thought this book was about balance. Why does it feel like I'm the kid on the seesaw, flailing my arms and legs, stuck in the air?"

I want to challenge you to see that the balance in this chapter is not about everything being even—it's about finding equilibrium between God's purpose for your life and plans.

I would go as far as to say that it's often easier for people to accept Christ as their Savior than it is to accept the plan God has for them because of that salvation.

There's a song written by Kelly Carpenter in January 1994 called "Draw Me Close." The lyrics say:

Draw me close to You.
Never let me go.
I lay it all down again,
Just to hear You say that I'm Your friend.

You are my desire.
No one else will do.
Because nothing else could take Your place,
To feel the warmth of Your embrace.
Help me find the way.
Bring me back to You.

The song goes on to say, "You're all I want."

When you truly find that place in His presence, you discover that what you need more than your personal plan is a personal relationship with Him.

TRUST IS ROOTED IN RELATIONSHIP

I believe part of our struggle with yielding our hearts to God is rooted in the depth—or lack thereof—of our relationship with Him. When there is no weightiness to your relationship with God, yielding becomes nearly impossible.

Jesus would send everyone away just to spend time with the Father. He was fully aware that to accomplish the purpose and plan set before Him, He would need time in His presence.

The Bible says, "For the joy that was set before Him, He endured the cross." Jesus was able to fulfill God's purpose because of the joy that was set before Him. And where is joy found? In God's presence. The Bible also says, "The joy of the Lord is your strength."

You only truly get joy when you are in the presence of God. It's while you are with Him that He infuses you with the strength to walk through the hardest parts of your life.

REFINING YOUR DREAMS AND DESIRES

So, you may ask, "What about my plans? My desires? My thoughts? My opinions? What do I want to get out of life?"

If you spend enough time with God, your desires don't die; they simply become refined. I don't believe that God kills dreams; I believe He refines them.

It's like a photographer who takes time with each image, removing blemishes to produce something aesthetically beautiful. So, it is with God and our plans. He doesn't burn down our desires; He filters them, so they are tried and true.

God wants you to be happy. But I believe He wants to filter your happiness through His divine system, so it is without spot or blemish. The Word says, "The blessing of the Lord makes rich, and He adds no sorrow with it."

This scripture highlights that it's possible to be wealthy and yet be filled with sorrow. But you bypass that pain when you first put your trust in God. When you follow His plan, place your desires in His hands, and allow Him to refine them, you gain something sustainable and pure.

BALANCE BUILDER · · · · · · · · · · · · · · · · · ·

Yielding is the soil where purpose grows. A yielding heart trusts God even when the journey feels uncertain. When you say "yes," you unlock doors not only for yourself but for others connected to your obedience. Choose to yield. It's where true balance begins.

Balance sometimes feels like imbalance. Especially when you're called to yield. These questions will help you examine your posture before God and inspire you to say "yes" even when it costs you something.

1. Where in my life have I been delaying a "yes" that God is patiently waiting for?

2. What fears or sacrifices are keeping me from fully surrendering to God's plan?

3. How have I misunderstood the purpose behind God's calling for my life?

4. In what ways do I need to build trust in God's character so I can say "yes" even without answers?

5. How can I daily yield my will, refine my desires, and walk boldly in obedience?

CHAPTER 7

WALKING IN FORGIVENESS

. . . .

THE WAR WITHIN

One of the phrases I hear so often is, "You don't know what they did to me." My intention in this chapter is not to exhaust every biblical, psychological, or life-coaching strategy to create a new you. My purpose here is simple: I want to address the war that rages within your mind. The one that keeps you from sleeping at night, that hinders you from loving at your highest capacity, that steals peace from your present, and that locks up parts of you that are meant to be free.

I'm not interested in clichés like, "Forgiveness is not for them; it's for you." Not that I don't believe it, but right now I believe there is something deeper we can tap into, an anointing to forgive.

When you've experienced deep hurt from those closest to you, it takes a heavy smearing of God's virtues to escape the enslavement of unforgiveness. I look around and see people living in their dungeons, locking themselves away in psychological basements, giving the green light to endless grief that haunts them day and night.

When I speak of a heavy smearing of God's virtues, I mean a literal saturation—a baptism—in the very essence of who God is. One of these virtues is revealed in Scripture, *"For God so loved the world that He gave His only begotten Son, that whosoever believeth in Him should not perish but have everlasting life."*

God showed the highest level of sacrifice to display the highest level of love—by giving His only Son for a world that is often flaky. If it were me, I wouldn't have considered it. Maybe, just maybe, for someone I knew would genuinely convert. But for a world where a high percentage would reject His gift? And then you have those who convert but still give only part of themselves to God while holding onto the world with the other half. I wouldn't have even been slightly interested.

Yet, God did it.

A HEAVY SMEARING OF VIRTUE

Heavy smearing of God's virtues is when His characteristics are poured over our hearts so deeply that we begin to see life from a different perspective. Jesus, while on the cross, gasping for breath, mustered up the strength to say, "Father, forgive them, for they know not what they do."

At the height of His pain and suffering, He found the grace to intercede for those who mocked Him, betrayed Him, denied Him, and disrespected Him. These are the virtues of God—unmistakable in their purity and undeniable in their power. These are the virtues we need to walk in when it comes to forgiving those who have wronged us.

THE POWER OF APOLOGIZING

Have you ever apologized when you weren't the one in the wrong? How did you feel? Did you feel noble, strong, or accomplished? If I'm honest, I didn't. I didn't feel victorious; I felt humbled.

Offering an apology—a genuine apology—for even the slightest glimpse of restoration is rewarding, but it's also painfully challenging. There is power in apologizing. There is power in admitting when you are wrong. And there is power in forgiving those who have hurt you.

But let's not pretend—it ranks among the most difficult decisions a person can make.

WHAT IS THE DESTINATION OF FORGIVENESS?

The destination of forgiveness is proper healing. If you know me as a pastor or a friend, you may have heard this story before. I had a bout with unforgiveness. I was arrogant enough to believe that I was healed and okay until I decided to go into prayer with God.

It was impressed upon me to pray for someone who had harmed me. Now, trust me, the infraction warranted prayer. But I'm not talking about a quick 30-second prayer. I'm talking about the kind of prayer that your old Baptist grandmother would pray—a "my family member is on life support, and I need God to move" kind of prayer.

I'm talking about a Holy Ghost-filled mother from the Church of God in Christ who knows how to grab ahold of the horns of the altar and wail until something shifts. That's the kind of prayer I needed.

A HEART BLOCKED AND BROKEN

I was operating on fumes, still doing life, but I felt like someone walking around with a 90% blockage in my heart. I was alive, but I was half dead. When I got on my knees and began to extend myself spiritually to God, I heard Him say, "Before you pray for anything, you need to pray for a pure heart."

I was immediately taken aback. I knew I was hurt, but I didn't realize I was injured. I didn't recognize that hatred had gripped me. Later, I would discover that I was so overwhelmed with hatred that I was a ticking time bomb—seconds away from imploding and exploding.

I was reckless. I was numb. The words of those closest to me had no effect. I was in a deep, dark place—feeling like Angela Bassett in *Waiting to Exhale* when she set her husband's belongings on fire and watched the car go up in flames. If you know, you know. I was out of control.

I'm describing this for you because, although my situation may not be your situation, rock bottom is still rock bottom. If I'm standing on the edge of a skyscraper, and you're standing next to me with the same contemplation to jump, I would say that both of our situations are painful. Different circumstances, same torment.

So, I decided to pray. And God hit me with a command I wasn't expecting, "Pray for a pure heart before praying for anything else."

Unforgiveness can express itself in ways so random and undetectable that anyone in your presence becomes unsafe. One of the reasons you must deal with unforgiveness is that you are highly contaminated. Something is altered in you that is altering everything around you.

You think you're just living life. In reality, everyone you come into contact with is being affected because the unforgiveness that rests in you seeps out into the atmosphere.

If I'm being transparent, I was so lost that I didn't care about anyone's opinion. It didn't matter who you were or what you had to say—I couldn't hear it. I was a mixture of grief, remorse, hate, regret, unforgiveness, anger, frustration, apathy, and spiritual numbness.

But in prayer—as I began to pray for God to purify my heart—He began to cleanse me. I want to describe that cleansing as a liberation. The Bible says, "Create in me a clean heart, O God, and renew a right spirit within me." God did that for me, and it set me up to be able to pray freely for the person who had wronged me.

Although there was still work to be done on my journey to forgiveness, praying for a pure heart created acceleration in that process.

I want to pass this suggestion on to you: **Before you pray for anything else, if you are living in a place of unforgiveness, pray that God will purify your heart.**

FORGIVENESS UNDER FIRE

In the seventh chapter of Acts, Stephen prayed for the people who were stoning him. I often meditate on this Scripture, trying to comprehend Stephen's level of tact, intuition, and focus while under such extreme attack.

The Bible says that, while Stephen was being stoned, he kneeled and cried with a loud voice, "Lord, lay not this sin to their charge." Then, he died.

Stephen's last words were sentiments injected with intercession and forgiveness.

How did Stephen find this level of balance—mentally, emotionally, psychologically, and physically—in a moment where people's voices were so loud that it would have been hard to hear his own?

How do you forgive when the volume of the hurt you've experienced is screaming so loudly that it overwhelms your willingness to forgive?

I believe that all of us, deep down, know that we should forgive. But because of the magnitude of the pain we endured, it causes a pause in our desire to do so.

TWO PRACTICAL MOVES
TOWARD FORGIVENESS

I want to give you two practical moves that I believe are critical in helping you walk in forgiveness.

If you break up the word forgive, you get two words: for (fore) and give. In other words, to give something before.

I suggest that before you ever stand face-to-face and toe-to-toe with someone's mishandling of you, you take a moment and start filling your emotional bank with spiritual currency.

So, before the hurt ever gets there, you have enough spiritual currency in your emotional bank to make a withdrawal without going bankrupt. The Bible says, "Thy word have I hid in my heart, that I might not sin against thee."

You must constantly be adding spiritual currency—Scripture, wisdom, encouragement, devotionals, conversations with mentors—into your emotional bank. So, when someone comes along and hurts you, you have enough spiritual currency stored up to not lose heart.

You are constantly repairing and preparing your heart for whatever may come.

PREPARE BEFORE
THE PROBLEM ARRIVES

What we know for sure is that problems will come. But if your heart is in the right place before the problem arrives, you will have the capacity to handle it appropriately.

You must understand that anything can happen. Those we love the most can sometimes hurt us the most. There is an art to this, and it looks like this:

> God, today I want You to teach me how to forgive
> in a way that honors You, heals me, and restores
> broken relationships. Lead me to Scriptures, lead

me to testimonies, and put me in the company of people who have an anointing to forgive.

This prayer predates your problem. This prayer does not subconsciously attract tribulation; it prepares you and anoints you so that when the enemy shows up, you're already covered.

THE POWER OF SPIRITUAL DEPOSITS

How do you think Stephen was able to forgive those who were stoning him? It was because he was full of the Holy Ghost. His emotional bank was filled with so much spiritual currency that, no matter what the enemy presented, he could only respond with what he had deposited.

If I go to a machine that dispenses coins for paper money, and the only coins I deposit are quarters, then no matter how much paper money I put in, the machine will only dispense quarters. It cannot produce dimes, nickels, or pennies because I never deposited them.

So, it is with our emotional bank. If we fill our emotional bank constantly with spiritual currency—wisdom, love, peace, and forgiveness—then when infractions come, our response will be what we have already deposited into our hearts.

Stephen could only respond to the people's hate with love because he kept spiritual currency in his emotional bank. Just like Stephen, we can't expect to respond with grace if we haven't been storing it up. You can't pour out what you haven't first put in.

PRAY FOR THOSE WHO HURT YOU

This last practical move is the most powerful one. In Matthew 5:44, Jesus instructs, *"Love your enemies and pray for those who despitefully misuse you."*

Balance is your ability to house certain emotions and still maintain control, so you don't lose focus on God's purpose for your life. If that is your end goal, you must learn to pray for those who mean you harm.

Can you lean into that uncomfortable place and pray for someone who hurt you? I desire for you to learn to lean into those tough spaces and pray until something shifts.

FORGIVENESS THROUGH PRAYER

Stephen kneeled and cried with a loud voice as he was being stoned—he interceded for those who wanted him dead. Jesus, on the cross, interceded for those who wanted to see Him crucified.

Your most powerful spiritual weapon that leads to total forgiveness is prayer. But not just any prayer—prayer for the person who hurt you.

To make this decision requires a leap of faith. Whatever the hurt is, it can be healed in prayer. I have witnessed it in my own life. God can heal you, speak to you about those who hurt you in a way that honors them, and sometimes—if it is His will—restore the relationship.

I don't believe God always intends for there to be reconciliation, but I do believe He desires for you to find healing and walk in true forgiveness.

I must be honest with you—praying for your enemy is not easy. I have offered this option to people, and many have declined. They just couldn't do it. I believe God knows exactly where you are. Maybe you can't do it today—but maybe tomorrow. It's a process.

I am a living witness that you will never truly be healed or able to forgive without this step. There were times when I was praying and crying because my heart was so broken. If you ever muster up the audacity to pray for your enemy, you may experience the same thing. But the only way up is through.

THROUGH PRAYER: THE ELEVATOR TO HEALING

Prayer is like an elevator. When you step in, the longer you stay, and the higher you can go. The more you trust God in that space, the more He will reveal to you, and the less of a grip that your pain will have on your life.

It's not instantaneous—it's a journey. But the higher you go, the clearer things become. Your vision changes and the weight of that pain starts to lift.

LET IT GO

I've contemplated and truly brooded over why God would allow forgiveness to be the final chapter. As we are landing this plane, God wants the message to be released: **You must let it go.**

Letting go does not mean you forget. But letting go frees you up to make choices that can change the trajectory of your life.

Start filling your emotional bank. Ease into praying for those who have hurt you, and you will find it easier to let it go. I don't believe God is looking for perfection. What He is looking for is action.

Faith in action is taking steps toward your healing so that you can be free.

LEARNING TO LET GO

When I was younger, I had a tooth extracted. After the procedure, the dentist packed it with gauze. They told me to continue putting pressure on that area to stop the bleeding. It was a molar, way in the back, and I clamped my teeth down to secure the gauze.

I held it there, biting down to make sure it stayed in place. But after some time, I started experiencing sharp, excruciating, throbbing pain. I assumed something was wrong. I thought maybe I had developed a dry socket because the pain just wouldn't stop.

I kept changing the gauze and clamping down hard, thinking I was following instructions. But the pain never left. I didn't realize that my continuous clamping down was creating the very pain I was feeling. For several hours, I endured that throbbing, convinced that something was terribly wrong, only to discover that my position was causing the pain.

The moment I removed the gauze, I experienced relief. The throbbing stopped. It was only after I decided to do something different that I finally felt the healing begin.

CHANGE YOUR POSITION

Could it be that the pain in your life has been sustained because you've never changed positions? Is it possible that you are creating your own discomfort by clamping down on something you were supposed to release?

It's time for you to do something you haven't done before. Either way, I needed to heal from the extraction, but I realized that I was causing myself more pain because of how I held on.

Whether you heal or not, the need for healing remains. But the process doesn't have to be accompanied by self-inflicted pain.

GIVE YOURSELF A BREAK

Your decision not to forgive, not to add spiritual currency to your emotional bank, and not to pray for the one who harmed you is equivalent to self-inflicted pain. Give yourself a break.

Stop clamping down on an area that needs to be released so you can experience relief. Let yourself live again. Let yourself love again.

It is my sincere desire that this chapter at least starts the process of healing for you. I can't imagine what you've experienced over your lifetime and what you've had to endure.

But what I do know is that you can find balance in your life—between what was harmful and what will produce healing. Healing is available to you.

Well, family, together, we have reached the final pages of this book. Two years ago, it was swirling around in the confines of my heart, and now it has taken form. I remember first sharing this book idea with a colleague who was a librarian during my last year as an educator. I recall sharing with her that writing this book weighed heavily on my heart. As I expressed and conceptualized my thoughts, she concurred that its impact would be powerful. Everyone I shared my sentiments with urged me to complete this book, as they felt that the world needed its content.

If you don't leave with anything else, I want you to feel a sense of urgency to keep fighting. The expectation is not perfection but a strive to be intentional about becoming a more balanced individual who knows how to thrive while encountering a plethora of challenges. I have a good friend whom I would always say to, "You got this!" He would be in the middle of a battle, and it would just come out of me. I couldn't help but say, "Bro, you got this!" I have watched him grow, blossom, and become a force to reckon with in the Kingdom of God. He had it, and he didn't know it. I want you to know, "You got this!"

Every chapter was explicitly designed to deal with an area in you that, if sharpened, you will be unstoppable, and you, too, will be a force to reckon with. I want this book to become a staple in your life and a reminder that when life gets hard, you will fight harder. Never let life outwork you. Be resilient! Be confident! Be bold! Be, well…balanced.

BALANCE BUILDER · · · · · · · · · · · · · · · · · ·

Forgiveness isn't forgetting—it's choosing to heal. When you release the grip of offense, you make space for God's peace. Prayer becomes your elevator out of pain and into freedom. Letting go is hard, but it leads to wholeness and balance.

Forgiveness is freedom. Reflect on these questions and invite God to help you unlock the healing power of release.

1. Who do I need to forgive—and what is that forgiveness tied to?

2. What has withholding forgiveness cost me emotionally or spiritually?

3. How can I begin the process of praying for the person who hurt me?

4. What would freedom look like if I finally let it go?

5. What would it mean to forgive myself and walk in grace?

A CLOSING PRAYER FOR HEALING, PROSPERITY, AND FORGIVENESS

Father, I thank You for Your anointing, the anointing that destroys every yoke and breaks every chain in our lives.

You said in Your Word that You desire for us to prosper and be in good health. So right now, I pray prosperity and true healing over every individual reading this prayer. Help them to walk through the process of forgiveness. Help them to find comfort in the uncomfortable, so that they may finally experience relief from the burden of unforgiveness.

I pray that they would have the spirit of Jesus and the spirit of Stephen—who both interceded for those who hurt them. Teach us, Father, to fill our emotional banks with spiritual currency, so that when new hurt arrives, there is enough grace deposited within us to extend to others.

Thank You, God, for every abundant and bountiful blessing You have bestowed upon us. As we rest and find peace through revelation, knowledge, and the awareness of Your presence, let us be unified and strengthened by our brothers and sisters in Christ.

Let there be balance in our lives. Help us not to shy away from the challenges, but to recognize that, with every challenge, there lies another opportunity to grow and flourish.

In Your mighty and matchless name, we pray, amen.

ACKNOWLEDGMENTS

First, I give all glory to God, the One who carried me through every uncomfortable season and helped me discover the balance that only He can provide.

To my wife, Tiffany, and our children, Kaalyn, Ty, and Matthew: you have been my sounding board, my constant support system, and my greatest encouragers. You have seen the ebbs and flows of my life, yet your confidence in me has never wavered. Your love, strength, and belief in me have anchored me through every season, and I am forever grateful for the joy and purpose you bring to my life.

To my mother, Brenda Mitchell: thank you for being my biggest cheerleader. Your love, encouragement, and unwavering belief in me have strengthened me more than words can express.

To my father, Pastor Ernest Mitchell, and my bonus mom, First Lady Debbie Mitchell: thank you for laying the foundation of ministry in my life and modeling faithful service to God. I am forever grateful for the years I spent under your leadership, serving as a musician, minister of music, youth pastor, and more. Your example and guidance have shaped the man, minister, and mentor I have become.

To Bishop Kevin Dickerson and Pastor Sonjia Dickerson: thank you for your covering, wisdom, and the spiritual leadership you provided during my 14 years in your ministry. You challenged me to grow in new ways and encouraged me to walk boldly in my calling.

To the Intersection Church family: thank you for trusting the vision God placed in my heart and walking alongside me as we build something meaningful and Spirit-led.

To all my family and friends who have supported me with prayer, encouragement, and love, you are deeply appreciated. Though too numerous to name, please know your impact on my journey has been profound.

Finally, to every reader navigating discomfort and transition, this book is for you. May it speak life to your situation and lead you toward the balance God has prepared for you.

ABOUT THE AUTHOR

Timothy Mitchell is a husband, father, pastor, educator, and entrepreneur. He is the founder and lead pastor of Intersection Church in Denton, Texas — a ministry where the heart of the people connects with the Heart of God.

Timothy's journey in ministry began under the leadership of his father, Pastor Ernest Mitchell, where he served faithfully for over a decade in various roles including musician, minister of music, and youth pastor. Later, he spent 14 years under the spiritual leadership of Bishop Kevin Dickerson, growing in both spiritual maturity and ministerial leadership.

With over 14 years of experience in education and administration, Timothy brings both structure and heart to every space he enters. He's passionate about helping others thrive in their faith, purpose, and personal growth. His entrepreneurial spirit is expressed through real estate, writing, and community-focused outreach.

Balance: The Journey to Becoming Comfortable in the Uncomfortable is Timothy's debut book — a deeply personal reflection on how God uses discomfort, delay, and detours to develop us for greater purpose.

www.ingramcontent.com/pod-product-compliance
Lightning Source LLC
Chambersburg PA
CBHW031443120626
46545CB00006B/2531